Walking in the Way

John Tallach

Christian Focus Publications Ltd.

Published by
Christian Focus Publications Ltd.
Geanies House
Fearn, Tain
Ross-shire IV201TW

© April 1983

ISBN 0 906731 28 3

Printed in Great Britain by
Bookmag, Henderson Road, Inverness IV1 1SP

And an highway shall be there, and a way, and it shall be called The way of holiness; the unclean shall not pass over it; but it shall be for those: the wayfaring men, though fools, shall not err therein.

No lion shall be there, nor any ravenous beast shall go up thereon, it shall not be found there; but the redeemed shall walk there . . .

Isaiah 35:8-9

Jesus saith unto him, I am the way . . .

John 14:6

Jesus is the Way, and there is no way to the Way; and if there be a door, Christ himself is the Door — and the door is open.

Adolph Saphir

Acknowledgements

Fear and Faith contains a quotation from p.244 of the *Biography of James Hudson Taylor*, pub. by the Overseas Missionary Fellowship. The O.M.F. hold the copyright of this book, and thanks are due to them for permission to use this quotation.

The Gospel contains a quotation from p.26 of *The Life and Labours of Duncan Matheson*, by John Macpherson, pub. by John Ritchie, Kilmarnock.

There is a River contains a quotation from p.200 of *John G. Paton, Missionary to the New Hebrides* — an autobiography edited by James Paton, pub. by The Banner of Truth Trust.

He Leadeth Me refers to incidents which are described on pp.214-5 of *From the Pulpit to the Palm Branch*: A Memorial of C.H. Spurgeon, pub. by Passmore and Alabaster.

Walking in the Way

*And an highway shall be there . . . and it shall be
called the way of holiness.*

Isaiah 35:7

No doubt Isaiah is referring here to the deliverance of
the Jews from bondage in Babylon. But his words may
also be taken to refer to the deliverance from sin which
all God's people experience, to the way in which they
walk through this world, and to their ultimate arrival at
their heavenly home.

What is the way in which Christians walk through
this world? Christ says 'I am the way'. Once in that
Way, it is in a sense impossible to go out of it. But in
another sense it is possible to wander from Christ. That
is where the danger lies for pilgrims — going out of the
Way. Out of the Way is where the lions and the
ravenous beasts are. They are prowling up and down
beside the Way, and the Way itself is the only place
where they cannot come.

There are many Christians walking along this Way.
But one of the tactics Satan uses to discourage pilgrims
is, to make them feel alone. This was how a Scottish
soldier felt one night, when he was in the trenches in
France during the First World War. He prayed to God
that he might meet even one with whom he could have
gospel fellowship. Shortly after that he heard a voice in
the darkness. He made his way to where a comrade lay
dying in a shell hole. He was just in time to hear this

man's last words, taken from Psalm 143:

> *Lo, I do stretch my hands*
> *To thee, my help alone;*
> *For thou well understands*
> *All my complaint and moan.*

It was just a step or two of the Way that they walked together, but the soldier's spiritual loneliness was gone. He had received the kind of encouragement of which John speaks: 'If we walk in the light, as he is in the light, *we have fellowship one with another*, and the blood of Jesus Christ his Son cleanseth us from all sin.'

Are we discouraged because of past wanderings from the Way, or because of present weakness in it? Let us look towards those who have passed along this Way, who have now been received into Heaven. The Bible does present them as those who have overcome; but it does not point to their constancy as the ultimate reason for their safe arrival in Heaven. Rather 'they washed their robes, and made them white in the blood of the Lamb. *Therefore* are they before the throne of God.' It was the blood of the Lamb which took them to the heavenly Jerusalem. Does it not have the power to carry you there too?

> *The ransomed of the Lord shall return, and come to Zion with songs and everlasting joy upon their heads: they shall obtain joy and gladness, and sorrow and sighing shall flee away.*

Waiting for God

Blessed are all they that wait for him.

Isaiah 30:18

What does this waiting mean? It does not mean that believers are just waiting around, doing nothing, vaguely hoping that something will turn up.

This waiting for God goes to the heart of the sinner's relationship with his Saviour, as Psalm 130 shows. All the elements in waiting for God are there. The Psalmist has learned that he has no resources of his own to meet his need: 'If thou, Lord, shouldest mark iniquities, O Lord, who shall stand?' He knows, too, that what he lacks himself, God has: 'But there is forgiveness with thee.' To that grace of God alone he looks: 'I wait for the Lord, my soul doth wait, and in his word do I hope. My soul waiteth for the Lord more than they that watch for the morning.' What a picture of the soul who has learned his lostness, his weary face turned towards the mercy of God, waiting for it to shine on him through Jesus Christ!

Waiting for God also expresses the relationship between a believer and his Lord. What was the spirit in which David went to fight Goliath? *Waiting for God*. 'I come to thee in the name of the Lord of Hosts . . . this day will the Lord deliver thee into my hand.' Going down into that valley, David could have sung to himself what he was afterwards to write:

My soul, wait thou with patience
upon thy God alone;
On him dependeth all my hope
and expectation.

And when he came up from that victory he could have sung, out of his own experience, to the watching Israelites:

Wait on the Lord, and be thou strong,
and he shall strength afford
Unto thine heart; yea, do thou wait
I say, upon the Lord.

Our relationship with God will be tried, too. We may take encouragement as we remember that trials can lead to a deepening in our relationship with God. But this will only happen if, throughout these trials, we wait for God. As John MacRae once said to believers sitting at the Lord's table, 'Your trials are like a strong wind blowing on a goodly tree. Not only will the force of adversity give exercise to all your graces, the result of which will be more fruitfulness; but it will also cause you to bow your head in Christian resignation. In such storms the dead tree will break, but not those who have in them the sap of grace.'

If we live in this spirit of dependence on the grace of God, even death itself will be turned into a great blessing. As Dr. Hugh Gillies said, 'Christ has so altered death in respect of the believer that it is just as if it were an invitation, *Come this way to Glory.*'

Revive thy Work

When he is come, he will convince the world of sin, and of righteousness, and of judgment.

John 16:8

Satan seems to triumph so easily today, and the church which should be looking for victories over him seems in no condition to fight. As a result of this, some Christians feel that the best they can hope for is a successful holding operation. They feel that, if they can only defend 'the faith once delivered to the saints', they will do well.

One could reply to this that the best form of defence is attack. Yet, however one might discuss strategy in this way, the important thing is that Scripture constantly points us to God's power in the face of our weakness. One of the Scriptures which did this for me recently in regard to revival was: 'And when he is come, he will convince the world of sin, and of righteousness, and of judgment: Of sin, because they believe not on me; Of righteousness, because I go to my Father, and ye see me no more; Of judgment, because the prince of this world is judged.'

The best preaching in the world cannot by itself convince of sin. But 'when he is come, *he* will convince the world of sin'. There can be no revival unless sinners will be convinced, not only that their works provide no basis for their justification, but also, positively, that they *can* be justified on the basis of the righteousness of

Christ. Who is to lead them into this gospel truth? 'When he is come *he* will convince the world of righteousness.' These are truths which the world of lost sinners needs to know, and the coming of the Spirit will manifest these truths to them.

The third truth which the Spirit will bring with power is one which relates more to those who already believe. How can there be revival unless the church of Christ, so weak and languishing just now, recaptures something of that note of victory which ought to characterise her witness? So, 'when he is come he will convince the world of judgment . . . because the prince of this world is judged.' The Spirit will show the church the completeness of Christ's victory over sin, and he will carry that victory over into the church's conscious experience. He will make them 'more than conquerors' through Jesus Christ.

It is not that the Spirit will come to give fresh revelations. It is not therefore that revival preaching will contain anything absolutely new. But he will convince the world of what has already been told; the proclamation of old truths will be accompanied by a new and irresistible power.

How we ought to pray for such revival, though we will expose ourselves to the attacks of Satan by so doing. How unitedly we ought to pray for it, so that what may be suffered by some will be shared by all. How earnestly we ought to pray for it, for the glory of our God is involved.

Revive thy work, O Lord.

Archippus

*And say to Archippus, Take heed to the ministry which
thou has received in the Lord, that thou fulfil it.*

Colossians 4:17

Paul himself does not seem to have planted the church
in Colosse; although he seems to have known some of
the believers there. Archippus was one of these believers. Perhaps he was one of those in Asia who, during
Paul's ministry in Ephesus, first 'heard the word of the
Lord Jesus' (Acts 19:10). That Paul knew Archippus is
confirmed by the reference in the letter to Philemon:
'Archippus our fellow soldier'.

What was Archippus thinking about, as he walked
along to the meeting house in Colosse, the day Paul's
letter was to be read? Was he praying, as Paul before
him, 'Lord, what wilt thou have me to do?' Or was he
harassed by temptation, doubting his call to Christ's
service, and thinking of giving up?

We can imagine the scene at the meeting house.
Paul's letter is read. The hearers are led to great heights
of Christian thought; they are also made to feel again
the practical demands which their faith places upon
them. They are reminded of their fellow Christians in
the neighbouring cities of Laodicea and Hierapolis.
Now, as Archippus looks at the elder reading the letter,
it seems that the letter has come to an end. There
remains only the customary parting greeting from the
apostle.

But there is something more to be said. 'And say to Archippus, take heed to the ministry which thou hast received in the Lord, that thou fulfil it.' If Archippus had been doubting whether his calling had been of God, he had no reason to doubt any more.

If he had been feeling that he had already discharged the responsibilities of his calling, that perhaps he should change to another sphere of labour, he could put these thoughts away now. There was no escape. It had even been publicly stated before the other believers that Archippus just had to face his calling and fulfil it.

As Archippus walked away from the meeting, was there anything in the rest of this Epistle that might have come to his mind, strengthening him for his task? '*Ye are complete in him*' (2:10). And as regards the spirit in which he should work, was there any word about that? 'And whatsoever ye do, do it heartily, as to the Lord, and not unto man; knowing that of the Lord ye shall receive the reward of the inheritance: for ye serve the Lord Christ' (3:23-24).

That meeting house is no more; Archippus and the other believers in Colosse have long since gone. But there are still believers in the world, and still some who have been called to serve in a special way. Perhaps these words have a message for one of them today: 'Take heed to the charge which thou hast received in the Lord, that thou fulfil it.'

Grieving the Spirit

And grieve not the Holy Spirit of God.

Ephesians 4:30

God cannot be hurt as we can be; and yet it was the Spirit himself who chose to express the command in such human terms: *Grieve not the Holy Spirit.* On the human level, the closer the relationship the deeper the hurt. Remember that, although your dearest friend is very near, he does not come so close as this: 'He is with you, and shall be *in* you.'

You may have tended at times to become estranged from your friend up the hill, across the street, or down by the shop. Have you found that, when dealing with such matters, prevention is better than cure? It is better to take steps towards closer fellowship than to ignore a crack in a relationship, allowing the crack to grow into a deep divide. Such close fellowship does not simply mean avoiding things which we know will hurt a friend; it is much more positive than that. Neither can this Scripture command be reduced to a mere list of negatives. It is an appeal for a closer walk with God. What is it then, that will please the Holy Spirit?

Faith. 'Without faith it is impossible to please him.' This is not the kind of faith which consists in mere knowledge of theology. It involves a living relationship; a daily tasting to see that '*God is good: who trusts in him is blessed.*'

You will have plenty of opportunities to show

whether or not you want to please him. Carnal reason will say one thing, the word of God another; worldly ambition will point one way, the providence of God another. Are you going to walk the way of faith or not?

Faith *which worketh by love*. Surely it is most significant that, having referred to our relationship with the Spirit, Paul turns immediately to our relationship with one another: 'Let all bitterness, and wrath, and anger, and clamour, and evil speaking, be put away from among you, with all malice. And be ye kind one to another, tender hearted, forgiving one another, even as God for Christ's sake has forgiven you.' A living relationship with God is something which cannot but sweeten our relationship with others. If we have faith reaching up to God in heaven, we will have love reaching out to men on earth. We might be ready to think that we have wonderful faith, until we see its limitations in the light of this test. 'He that saith he is in the light, and hateth his brother, he is in darkness.' 'By this shall all men know that ye are my disciples, if ye have love one to another.' You say, 'But I cannot agree with that brother's views.' God does not necessarily ask you to agree with his views, but he does ask you to love him. Then you argue, 'But he is so arrogant.' God does not ask you to love your brother's faults, but to love himself.

Grieve not the Holy Spirit. He dwells in the other man, too. Through him you are members one of another, and he is working towards that heavenly day when the spiritual oneness of all believers will have the most open and glorious expression possible. Grieve not the Spirit who has such an end in view.

He saw Them

He saw them toiling in rowing.

Mark 6:48

There is a background to this incident. After the miracle of the loaves and fishes, the people had begun to talk of making Christ a king. Also, Mark tells us that the hearts of the disciples were hardened, so that they had not been duly affected by the miracle of the loaves. Maybe the disciples themselves were caught up in the excitement of the crowd, as they began to hope that Jesus would become an earthly king and would lead them to freedom from the Romans. Perhaps it was these carnal thoughts which hardened the disciples' hearts, and lost them the spiritual blessing from the miracle.

Whatever others thought of the crowd and the excitement as an opportunity for power and popularity, Jesus threw the opportunity away. He made the crowd disperse, and he 'constrained' his disciples to get into their boat and row towards the other side. That was how they met this storm. Throughout the long hours of darkness it raged — up to midnight and on till three o'clock in the morning. The disciples were tormented with rowing. They were far past the ordinary limits of mental and physical endurance.

Yet Christ did not come to help. The disciples might have felt, 'We thought that he cared for us, but how can he care for us when he leaves us here? It is all right for him on the land. Has he no concern for us tormented out here on the sea?'

No doubt they thought that Christ could not see them through the darkness. But he could see them very clearly.

As Job said when he felt himself walking in darkness, 'He knoweth the way that I take' (Job 23:10). And as David wrote, 'Thou hast considered my troubles; thou hast known my soul in adversities' (Psalm 31:7).

It might have *looked* as if he did not care, but this appearance was deceiving. For when he had sent his disciples out to meet the storm, he himself had gone up the hillside to pray. Surely every aspect of their circumstances was embraced in that prayer. The strength of the wind, the height of the waves, the safety of their bodies and souls — everything was covered by his intercession. They met a screaming wind, they were tossed by mountainous waves, but nothing could carry them beyond the reach of this: 'I pray for them'.

Then, sometime between three and six in the morning, he walked towards them on the waves. They did not recognise him at first. In fact, what was to prove their salvation in the end, served at first only to intensify their fear. But then he spoke: 'Be of good cheer: it is I; be not afraid.'

They had been brought to the point where they were willing to let all else go, if they could only have Christ himself. He could cross their wills as to how he would set up his kingdom, as long as they had him. How willingly then they reached out into the darkness when he spoke, and took him just as he was into the ship!

That was the turning point. There was outward and inward calm after that. In no time at all they arrived at what they had been striving for hopelessly all the night.

The Gospel

The gospel of the grace of God

Acts 20:24

Paul told the Galatians that he had not received the gospel from any man, 'but by the revelation of Jesus Christ'. He wrote to Timothy about 'the gospel of the glory of the blessed God'. For Paul, then, the gospel was of God in its origin and in its aim.

What is this gospel that comes from God and points us back to him? To the Ephesian elders at Miletus Paul described it as 'the gospel of the grace of God'. This is just another way of saying that the content of the gospel is divine as well. Had Paul preached to the Jews that they must save themselves, this would have been no news. Had he told the Gentiles that they must save themselves, this would have been no divine revelation to them. This had been man's religion since the fall. But what Paul preached was real news: that which Jews and Gentiles had failed to accomplish by religious observance or by natural wisdom, God had done in Christ. 'God was in Christ, reconciling the world to himself, not imputing their trespasses to them' (2 Cor. 5:19).

This is the gospel which Duncan Matheson, born last century in north east Scotland, was to take to the soldiers fighting in the Crimean War. But when he first became concerned about his own salvation, he did not know what this gospel meant. He was afraid of hell: he tried to please God as best he could. There were seventy steps to the lodgings in Edinburgh where he was staying at the time, and he used to send up a prayer to God at every step. He did not see that he was trying to climb to heaven by what he did himself. He looked for sympathy to one minister, but this minister said 'I see you are angry with God for not giving you salvation as a reward of works. But it must be grace from first to last.' Matheson tells what happened next in his own words:

I was standing, on the 10th December, 1846, at the end of my father's house, meditating on that precious word: 'God so loved the world, that he gave his only begotten Son, that whosoever believeth in him should not perish, but have everlasting life.' I saw that 'whosoever' meant anybody and everybody, and therefore me, even me. I saw the result of believing — that I would not perish, but have everlasting life. I was enabled to take God at his word. I saw no one but Jesus only, all in all in redemption. My burden fell from my back, and I was saved . . . I could not contain myself for joy. I sang the new song, salvation through the blood of the Lamb. The very heavens appeared as if covered with glory. I felt the calm of a pardoned sinner; yet I had no thought about my safety. I saw only the person of Jesus. I wept for my sin that had nailed him to the cross, and they were tears of true repentance. Formerly I had set up repentance as a toll between me and the cross; now it came freely as the tear that faith wept.

That is how the gospel came to mean everything to Duncan Matheson. It is the story, not of his giving to God, but of God's giving to him. Has it yet become 'the gospel of *the grace of God*' to us?

Time

To every thing there is a season, and a time to every purpose under heaven.

Ecclesiastes 3:1

It is one of the aspects of grace, that it brings creatures who are subject to the limits of time into living communion with God who inhabits eternity. The more they are living for God and for eternity, the more submissive they will be to the rigorous disciplines of time.

Only the gracious will seek God in time. 'For this shall everyone that is godly seek thee *in a time when thou mayest be found*.' By contrast, Christ foretold that the destruction of unbelieving Jerusalem would come 'because thou knewest not *the time of thy visitation*'.

Only the gracious will serve God in time. The people of Jerusalem were saying in Haggai's day, as they went in and out of their comfortable homes, 'The time is not come, the time that the Lord's house should be built.' But the word of God came to expose their hypocrisy: 'Is it time for you, O ye, to dwell in your cieled houses, and this house lie waste?' Mordecai was more alive to God's times and seasons in his day. He saw that Esther had been raised to her exalted position for 'such a time as this', and pressed her to use the opportunity to speak for the people of God. Mordecai knew the difference between 'a time to keep silence, and a time to speak'; he knew which of these times it was then. 'A wise man's heart discerneth time and judgment.'

But there are negatives as well as positives in that list in Ecclesiastes chapter 3. 'A time to plant, *and a time to pluck up that which is planted*; a time to get, *and a time to lose*; a time to keep, *and a time to cast away.*' What a negative it is to have to cease from a particular aspect of our service for Christ! 'A time to be born, *and a time to die.*' What a negative to have to stop our service for Christ altogether in this world! But if we are living in close communion with him who is above all limits of time, what will we say of death? '*He hath made everything beautiful in his time.*' Even death. For then, the time of greatest loss becomes the time of greatest gain, the supreme negative is turned into the ultimate positive. Absent from the body, present with the Lord.

Guidance

Lord, what wilt thou have me to do?

Acts 9:6

When Saul of Tarsus was brought down to the dust of the Damascus road his first prayer was, 'Lord, what wilt thou have me to do?' It is a vivid testimony to the fact that, when God takes possession of a soul for himself, that soul will then pray to be guided by God in all he does.

The question of guidance is not an easy one. No doubt Paul often afterwards prayed that same prayer, but how often was the answer so clear as it was on this occasion? It was not every day that he received an Ananias, sent to show him exactly what he should do. But there are some aspects of this first case which would more or less have featured in all future ones, and in the light of which we can examine ourselves today. There is first of all the sincere desire to be led. In that first prayer offered after his meeting with Christ, Saul expressed this gracious attitude. Before, he had driven others, he had sought to impose his will on them. Now he bowed before the Head of the church, asking to know *his* will.

Implicit in this prayer was the belief that God had a purpose for him. He had been shown his nothingness, he had been shown the emptiness of all his past activities. But still he looked up, expecting to be used. Surely this ought to be true of all God's children. They have been shown their emptiness, but they have also been shown the grace of God in Christ. Saved by his grace, should they not expect to be used to his glory?

The first part of the answer to Saul's prayer came in the words: 'Go into the city, and it shall be told thee what thou must do.' He did not receive a detailed answer immediately; he had to wait for it in faith. So the sincerity of our prayer, the reality of our faith, may also be tested as we wait for an answer in our own case. The Old Testament church had the guidance of God given her in a visible sign: 'And the Lord went before them by day in a pillar of cloud, to lead them the way, and by night in a pillar of fire, to give them light; to go by day and night' (Exodus 13:21). How can we fear that God's guidance will be less sure, though outwardly less visible, in this New Testament age? By his word and Spirit he will enlighten us, through fellow believers he will encourage us, by his providence he will lead us. In some, or in all of these ways he will fulfil his promise to those who wait for him:

I will instruct thee and teach thee in the way which thou shalt go.

Covetousness and Contentment

Let your conversation be without covetousness: and be content with such things as ye have: for he hath said, I will never leave thee, nor forsake thee. So that we may boldly say, the Lord is my helper, and I will not fear what man shall do unto me.

Hebrews 13:5-6

Do you have to work in an atmosphere which is frequently charged with industrial unrest? Then perhaps these words are for you. They are also for the mother, shopping with her children in a supermarket, who is unable to afford all she had hoped to buy. Again they have something to say to those whom God has placed above the straightened circumstances of others, but not above his word: 'Charge them that are rich . . . that they be not high minded, nor trust in uncertain riches, but in the living God.' The temptation is there for us all, particularly in these days of discontentment, to think that if we could only have that something *more* we would have perfect happiness.

Covetousness was a feature of that first sin by which we all fell. Did Adam not have enough in the Garden of Eden? He did not need the forbidden fruit; his grasping it was an act of pure rebellion against the word of God. What contrasting contentment the second Adam showed in the wilderness! Christ had the power to change the stones into bread, but he would not use that power. 'Man shall not live by bread alone, but by every word that proceedeth out of the mouth of God.' It was not the bread itself which was the important thing. Christ was looking rather to the word of God which appoints the means by which his creatures are sustained; the word which ruled all his own circumstances. He who made all things would not be induced by Satan to seek even bread, when it was clearly his Father's will that he should be without it. He was content with such things as he had.

I will not fear. As the unbeliever will not take God for his comfort, he is afraid. He is afraid that, what he has today, he will lose tomorrow. He is afraid that, in the race to acquire new standards of living, he will be left behind. Fear breeds quickly in a grasping, godless, world. In the last few years we have seen, through high rates of inflation, how suddenly our circumstances can change, how quickly comforts can be taken away. Have you had to give up some things, and are you wondering why God has not protected you from this? Perhaps he intends that someone, who may have earthly riches but is poor towards God, will look at your life in his calculating way and read this message there:

Godliness with contentment is great gain.

A Mountain with a View

In the mount of the Lord it shall be seen.

Genesis 22:14

Whatever our sphere of service, we can be sure that we will meet with difficulties. Abraham had a mountain to climb, and a heavy load to carry as he climbed it. He was concerned for Isaac personally, but he must have been more concerned because of God's word regarding him: 'In Isaac shall thy seed be called'. In being asked to slay his son, he was being called to cut off God's promise, to oppose his purposes, to throw his provision away.

What was it that gave Abraham strength to climb that mountain? *Faith*. 'God will provide himself a lamb for a burnt offering.' That was what gave him strength to carry on. 'God has a greater concern for the survival of his cause than I,' he thought. 'He has come under obligation to provide for its every need.'

How often we ask to see first, before we believe. Thomas said, 'Except I see . . . I will not believe.' But he had reversed the order of Scripture. As Jesus said to Martha, standing by her brother's tomb, 'Said I not unto thee that, if thou wouldest *believe* thou shouldest *see* the glory of God?' The day for seeing will come for all God's children; but as far as the time of testing is concerned they must go on in faith.

In a sense, although Abraham would not see everything fully for a long time, a preview of that day was not far away. Even in the entwining of the ram's horns in the branches of the thicket he could see that 'All things work together for good to them that love God, to them who are the called according to his purpose.'

What else did Abraham see on the mountain? *He saw my day, and was glad* (John 8:56). Abraham had given up his son at the call of God; but the sacrifice had not been needed in the end. Now Abraham looked, not on his own giving, but on the giving of God. He looked towards that giving which lies behind and above all the giving to which we will ever attain. 'God so loved the world, that he gave his only begotten Son, that whosoever believeth in him should not perish, but have everlasting life.'

What is the mountain that lies ahead in the work to which God has called you? Whatever it is, don't try to walk round it. Climb it in faith; and it will prove a place from which you, too, will see the glory and the grace of God.

Creation and Redemption

God did rest the seventh day from all his works . . . He that is entered into his rest, he also hath ceased from his own work, as God did from his. Let us labour therefore to enter into that rest.

Hebrews 4:4,10,11

As God rules in creation as well as redemption, it is natural that we find parallels between his work in the two realms.

The three Persons of the Godhead were seen at work in creation. God the Father created; but God the Son was involved too (John 1:3), as was the Holy Spirit (Genesis 1:2). As regards redemption, the involvement of the three Persons is seen, for example, in Jude 20-21.

In the succeeding days of creation, in the gradually increasing complexity of the world, it seems evident that, behind creation, there was a *plan*. We have to come to the same conclusion, too, when we look at the orderly development seen in the realm of redemption. In fact, in Ephesians 1:4, Paul says that the plan for the salvation of the church was laid down before the world itself was made.

But what is the use of a plan without *power*? And what breathtaking power lies behind the brief, bare statements in which the beginning of Genesis abounds: 'In the beginning God created the heaven and the earth . . . and God said, Let there be light: and there was light.' Paul draws an express parallel between the creation of light at the beginning and the experience of souls who are born again; 'For God, who commanded the light to shine out of darkness, hath shined in our hearts, to give the light of the knowledge of the glory of God in the face of Jesus Christ.'

Another point about God's work of creation is that it *provided rest*. The first day after Adam's creation was a day of rest. It was a day for celebration; a day when man was called simply to rest in the perfection of God's finished work. This aspect of the parallel between creation and redemption is drawn out expressly in Hebrews 4:9-10. As God did all the work of creation and asked man to rest in it, so Christ completed all the work of redemption, and calls sinners to rest in that. It is not for us to labour, but to lie down at the foot of the cross on which Christ laboured even to death; to rest our souls on the truth he proclaimed from that cross: *It is finished*.

When we cross that Line

Lo, this is our God: we have waited for him and he will save us: this is the Lord; we have waited for him, we will be glad and rejoice in his salvation.

Isaiah 25:9

Recently I attended the funeral of a colleague in the ministry. There was an inevitable sadness about the occasion, but there was a gladness too. Shortly before he died he was heard to say 'It won't be long now.' Psalm 23 was sung by those standing around his bed, and he tried to join in the singing. At the last verse he raised his hand and smiled; evidently he knew that these words had a special meaning for him. Only a few minutes later he passed from partaking in the praises of the church on earth to join in the song of the redeemed above.

One remarkable end about which the Old Testament tells us is Jacob's. The strenuous activity of his early years is finished. More significantly, the carnal striving after earthly gain has passed away. This is where he takes his stand now: 'I have waited for thy salvation, O Lord' (Gen. 49:18). He has come to realise that salvation is all of sovereign grace, and he has learned to wait in spiritual dependence on the Author of that salvation.

Perhaps the most beautiful end described in the New Testament is Stephen's. The murderous activity of his enemies is contrasted with the stillness in which 'he fell asleep'. The hatred which caused his enemies to cast him out of this world is contrasted with the love which moved the Saviour to stand and receive him into Heaven.

Whether it be sooner or later, 'what man is he that liveth and shall not see death?' Whether it comes suddenly as with Stephen, or peacefully as with Jacob, it will come. The great matter is to live in a spirit of total dependence on the grace of God, as these two did. For those who say on this side of death, 'I have waited for thy salvation, O Lord' will say when they cross that line:

Lo, this is our God; we have waited for him and he will save us: this is the Lord; we have waited for him, we will be glad and rejoice in his salvation.

Putting the gospel to Work

Occupy till I come.

Luke 19:13

One of the lessons of this parable must be that, as each servant received his pound from the nobleman, so every blessing we get is a gift from God through Christ. But what the parable teaches most emphatically is our duty to put the gifts of God to the utmost use. Now the gospel is God's greatest gift to us. In relation to the gospel, then, we must take heed to the crucial words in the parable, 'Occupy till I come'. The meaning of the term is: *Put the money to use — make it work.*

This is how we must approach the gospel, if we have not yet believed in Jesus Christ. When the crowds in Jerusalem were convicted under Peter's preaching they cried out 'What shall we do?' Peter's reply pointed them to Christ; he told them to repent and to believe in him. He was showing them how to put the gospel to work. When the Philippian jailer was aroused by the earthquake, he too asked 'What must I do to be saved?' Paul told him to believe in Jesus and be saved. He told him to use the gift of God — to put it to work. If he would only receive Christ, Christ would answer his question by doing the saving for him.

This must be the relationship between believers and the gospel to the end. The gospel is not something which the church receives, only to wrap it up. It is not to be insulated in fine ritual or in tradition or in fancy language. It is something which must be a living force in our hearts, *the* driving power in our lives. Is the gospel like that to us? If not, perhaps what we need is to remove whatever we have wrapped around it, and to put it to work.

In the earlier part of his Epistle to the Ephesians, Paul submits in the most unqualified way to the sovereignty of the grace of God. But in the latter part of the same Epistle, one senses his burning desire to see the gospel worked out in practical religion. He wants to see the Ephesian believers put the gospel to work in their *walk*; 'I beseech you that you walk worthy of the vocation wherewith ye are called.' Again, he wants to see believers put the gospel to use in *warfare*; 'Put on the whole armour of God . . . for we wrestle not against flesh and blood, but against the rulers of the darkness of this world.' Paul does not want the Ephesians to be like the man in the parable, ironically wrapping up his pound in a cloth intended to absorb the sweat of a labouring man. He wants them to put the gospel to work in all aspects of their daily living.

How long are we to labour like this? We do not know. All we know is that Christ has said to us, 'Occupy *till I come*.' When he comes again, and subjects our present use of the gospel to the closest scrutiny, what will he find?

All . . . for Good

*And we know that all things work together for good to
them that love God, to them who are the called
according to his purpose.*

Romans 8:28

Paul is not speaking of everyone here. He is referring to
those who, from God's perspective, are his *called*; and
who, from the human point of view, are *those who love
God*.

These people face trouble. Christ warned his disciples that they would meet trouble in the world. Paul
told new converts that 'we must through much tribula-
tion enter into the kingdom of God'.

Yet Paul writes, without any qualification, 'All
things work together for good'. Outward and inward
troubles; past, present and future; trouble that one
bears personally, and difficulties met with while serv-
ing Christ in the world — *all things*.

In the face of these difficulties, Paul sets this encouragement before believers. He points them past the
evil that they see to the good which God intends. And
he gives them a solid basis for this encouragement. He
does not direct them to their own feelings or experi-
ences, but to the unchangeable purposes of God.

Look at the purposes of God, says Paul, revealed in
Christ. How *publicly* God revealed his love to you, when
he sent his son to die for you on the cross. How can

anything now reverse the purposes God proclaimed so openly? How *personally* God's secret purposes have been opened up to you, in the work of his Spirit in your hearts! You may be groaning because of sin, but in these groanings themselves the Spirit of God is bearing witness that he lives in your heart.

When Thomas Hogg was chaplain in Dunrobin Castle, around 1653, he was one day so filled with happiness in prayer that he said, 'What would I not suffer for such unbounded goodness?' Just then he was called to take worship in the castle. To his dismay and embarrassment, all the comfort that he had been feeling suddenly vanished away. He could hardly pray at all. As Hogg left that room in the castle, the Countess of Sutherland whispered something to him 'Do not be discouraged,' she said. 'The Lord is trying your submission to his sovereign will.' Back in his room, Hogg was wondering why he had been called to go through this trying experience. Then he remembered what he had been saying in the midst of his previous comfort: 'What would I not suffer for this?' He saw that God had taken him at his word! Now he submitted to God's will, and his comfort came again. In telling this story, Hogg used to summarise the lesson he learned: 'Consolation pleases us, but submission pleases God'.

Submission requires self discipline — great denial of our own wisdom and wishes, and much cheerful faith. In a web of cloth, some strands are at right angles to others. They seem to be at cross purposes. And yet the cloth could not exist without both; the one strand holds the other strand in place. We are not able in our wisdom to see the broad pattern which God is weaving in our lives. We sometimes find ourselves staring distractedly at what seems to us to have no meaning at all. But we must rest in him who does see; and as we rest in him we become 'more than conquerors through him that loved us'.

We will soon see it plainly. But meantime we must say it in faith, whether we see it or not: *All things work together for good.*

Joy

Restore to me the joy of thy salvation.
Psalm 51:12

During his year of backsliding, David tasted the joys of sinful pleasures. But as he turned again to God, he set aside these other joys as unworthy of comparison with 'the joy of thy salvation'.

This is a joy in which heaven is involved. The angels rejoiced as they saw the Son of God go out into the world to seek the lost. They also rejoice to see sinners come back to God, as a fruit of Jesus' work: 'There is joy in the presence of the angels of God over one sinner that repenteth.' Surely a joy in which all heaven is involved must be the greatest joy that we can possibly know.

The joy of God's salvation flows from what God has done. Jesus illustrated this when he described the prodigal returning to his father and confessing his sin. The son had been active before, but all his activity had brought him misery. Now he just stands there in his rags, and his father sets things going on his behalf: 'Bring forth the best robe, and put it on him; and put a ring on his hand, and shoes on his feet; and bring hither the fatted calf, and kill it; let us eat and *be merry*'.

Join the eunuch's chariot, as he drives on through the desert to Ethiopia. Ask him why he is going on his way rejoicing, and he will reply: 'Surely he has borne my griefs and carried my sorrows . . . the Lord has laid on him my iniquities. How can I *not* rejoice, when God has done these things for me?'

The joy of God's salvation is a joy that is very deep. There is joy *in* the Holy Spirit (Romans 14:17); joy *of* the Holy Spirit (1 Thess. 1:6). Here is a joy of which the influences of the Spirit are an essential part — what joy can be deeper than that?

If we have not yet known this joy, let us ask God that we may know it now. Not that we wait around, simply hoping that the Spirit of God will somehow visit our hearts with this joy. It was because the Ethiopian eunuch believed in Jesus that he went on his way rejoicing. When we look to Jesus Christ to be the Saviour of our souls, we will know this joy too.

Perhaps we used to know this joy but have now lost it. Perhaps we lost it because we followed our own wills instead of asking, 'Lord, what wilt thou have me to do?' Or did we lose it because we sought out pleasures connected with some sinful thing? Whatever the reason, let us now pray as David did, 'Restore to me the joy of thy salvation'.

How can this joy be restored? 'Purge me with hyssop, and I shall be clean: wash me, and I shall be whiter than snow.' A godly woman who was under great temptation went to Thomas Hogg for advice. He told her to suppose for a moment that all the temptations she was presented with were true — and then to make application to the blood of Christ, to cleanse her from all sin. This was the means of restoring to her 'the joy of the Lord, which was her strength'.

There is still the same power in that blood. It is strong enough to beget in all who turn to it *the joy of thy salvation*.

The Laughter of Faith

Then Abraham fell upon his face, and laughed.
Genesis 17:17

What makes people laugh? Is it that we have an in-built sense of order, and that when a situation is presented to us which challenges that order, a tension is set up in our minds which finds relief in laughter? We laugh, that is, when we see the threat as an apparent one; if we see it as a real threat, we cry.

The background to the scene in which Isaac was named is filled with order. Abraham, as he wanders through a strange land, has his protection secured by the promise of God; 'Fear not, Abraham; I am thy shield, and thy exceeding great reward.' And as to his posterity, God showed him the stars and said, 'So shall thy seed be'. After that comes a period of at least thirteen years in which nothing happens, and nothing seems to be said. There is activity on the part of Sarah (chapter 16) in which she tries to relieve the situation by providing seed through her handmaid; but on the level of the covenant purposes of God, all seems at a standstill.

Then, after this period of waiting, God speaks again. He just takes up where he has left off, and elaborates on what he has said. Imagine a friend promising you something, and not speaking about it again for thirteen years. Then he meets you one day and says quite casually, 'I am now going to give you what I promised you'. Yet, although God renews his promise, nothing is done. Even after thirteen years, nothing is to happen immediately. There is the change of Abraham's name, pointing to the multitude of nations he is to bear, but the child through whom God's promise is to be fulfilled is not yet born! Here are two worlds brought into tense conflict — the certain ordered world from which God speaks, and the weak, childless, ageing world in which Abraham lives. The tension is so great that Abraham laughs. But he laughs because he believes. If in unbelief he had given prominence to the world of his weakness, he would have wept. Yet because in faith he held uppermost the world of God's promise and power, his tension found relief in laughter; and God set the seal of his approval on Abraham's response. 'God said, Sarah thy wife shall bear thee a son indeed; and thou shalt call his name Isaac' — *he laughs*.

The covenant purposes of God are still being fulfilled. If we have any part in their fulfilment, we too will sense the apparent incompatibility between the covenant world of perfect order and the world in which we live. If our response to God's promise is one of unbelief, our feelings will only find expression in tears of despair. But if we respond in faith, we will do what the father of the faithful did. 'Then Abraham *laughed*.'

There is a River

Though the earth be removed, and though the mountains
be carried into the midst of the sea; though the waters
thereof roar and be troubled, though the mountains
shake with the swelling thereof; there is a river, the
streams whereof shall make glad the city of God.

Psalm 46:2-4

It is obvious from this Psalm that believers are not exempt from trouble. Verses 2-3 speak of the earth being moved, of the mountains being swept into the sea; they paint a terrifying picture of disorder and chaos. It is also obvious that such troubles present a test of the church's faith, and uncover the source of her comfort.

The church's faith is not a wall which closes in a pool. The faith of believers is more like a channel which lets a river run through. Their consolation is not like stagnant water. Rather, the river of the grace of God is a refreshing, living thing.

The church is surrounded by trouble, but 'there is a river, the streams whereof shall make glad the city of God'. There is comfort, flowing to the church in the midst of her distress. The church is in the midst of trouble, but *God is in the midst of the church.*

There is a good illustration of this in the autobiography of John G. Paton who, in 1858, went as a missionary to the New Hebrides. At the time of this particular incident, he had already given his all towards establishing a mission on the island of Tana. His wife and infant son were buried there. But now the time had come to leave. Savages were searching for him, determined to take his life. He abandoned his home and hid in the branches of a tree, hoping to continue his escape when the moon rose.

We can imagine distressing thoughts filling his mind, as he crouched in the branches of that tree. Everything he had built up seemed to be falling apart; disorder was reigning, chaos was everywhere. Yet that is not how Paton remembered the scene:

> I heard the frequent discharging of muskets, and the yells of the savages. But yet I sat there among the branches, as safe in the arms of Jesus. Never, in all my sorrows, did my Lord draw nearer to me, and speak more soothingly in my soul, than when the moonlight flickered among these chestnut leaves, and the night air played on my throbbing brow, as I told all my heart to Jesus. Alone, yet not alone! If it be to glorify my God, I will not grudge to spend many nights alone in such a tree, to feel again my Saviour's spiritual presence, to enjoy his consoling fellowship.

Yes, there *is* a river, the streams whereof shall make glad the city of God.

Short Prayers

Remember me, O my God, for good.

Nehemiah 13:31

It is good that some of the most precious prayers in the Bible are very short; they are easy to remember.

When we feel our need of God's keeping, we can use David's prayer: *Lord keep me.* When we feel our need of help we should remember what the Syro-Phoenician woman said: *Lord, help me.* And when we feel our unworthiness, let us remember the publican's prayer: *God be merciful to me a sinner.*

Nehemiah could be regarded as the prophet of short prayers. The prayer that he offered between the king's question and his own answer could not have been very long. And later on, when caught up in the work of rebuilding Jerusalem, there was everything to maintain the brevity and pointedness of his prayers. The work he was doing was one of real worth — to the glory of God, and the good of his church in the world. There was no need for him to speak in an artificial way, trying to increase the impression of the importance of what he was saying. Nor did he need to multiply words, seeking to cover up spiritual barrenness or inactivity. There was a war on, and Nehemiah's prayers had the brevity of dispatches from the front line to Headquarters. In chapter 6:9, for example, he simply cries 'Strengthen my hands.'

During these eventful days, Nehemiah knew times of

sorrow and of joy. He wept at the thought of how Jerusalem lay desolate and dust laden. But he had to say, too, as the people in Jerusalem felt the power of the word of God, 'The joy of the Lord is your strength.' With his increased experience, did his prayers grow longer towards the end of his life? It does not seem so. It is on a characteristic note of personal pointed prayer that the record of his life comes to an abrupt end. The words are few, but the meaning takes in everything:

Remember me, O my God, for good.

No Turning Back

I will go in the strength of the Lord.

Psalm 71:16

It seems likely that David wrote this psalm, and that it was written on the occasion of Absalom's rebellion. If so David was meeting, at a late stage in his career, many things which were distressing and discouraging. They were calculated to turn him back; or, at least, to make him stop. They were certainly tending to make him say anything but these words, *I will go*.

David was old, and he was having to leave his throne, his home and his city. His enemies were filled with hatred towards him, and they planned to take his life (vs. 10-11).

Yet David was not taken up with these discouraging things. Even in a situation in which he was vulnerable, in which he seemed to be losing everything, he thought in a positive way. He remembered God's kindness in the past (vs. 5-6). Looking back to his birth, and to the years he had spent as a shepherd, he recognised how he had known the care of God. What then was the fruit of this? He realised that, though his circumstances had changed so dramatically, God had not. He still ruled in the details of his life. His power and grace were the same, and he would send deliverance yet (v. 20).

David would be delivered, his enemies would be confounded; but this itself was not the aspect of the future which David found most attractive. What excited David most was the prospect of having fresh reason to sing the praises of God. 'I will praise thee with the psaltery, even thy truth, O my God: unto thee will I sing with the harp, O thou Holy One of Israel. My lips shall greatly rejoice when I sing unto thee; and my soul, which thou hast redeemed' (vs. 22-23). It is not in turning back that we will get fresh strength. It is not while indulging a spirit of despondency that we will meet fresh reasons to sing God's praise. Difficulties and discouragements may seem to lie ahead. But surely there is reason for us, too, to say *I will go in the strength of the Lord*.

Fear and Faith

Be not afraid, only believe.

Mark 5:36

Fear is a problem which we face at every stage of life.

If our mother goes out of the room when we are young children, disappearing from the world which we see, we are afraid that we have lost her altogether. As we grow up, we are afraid of failing exams; or, perhaps, of not being successful in the football or the netball team. When we become adults, we are afraid of not coping with the stresses we meet at work, or of not being able to adapt to a new environment. When old age comes on and our friends die, we are still afraid. We feel that we are being left behind, stranded like a piece of driftwood on the beach. Yet we are also afraid to go.

How do we learn to substitute faith for fear? We must begin by realising that the source of fear is within ourselves. Fear is the fruit of sin. We must also realise that God, the only worthy object of our faith, is outside of us.

It was the sudden realisation of this that made the difference for the woman of Samaria. There was an apparent confidence in her prattling talk, but underneath was there not a nervous tension, a sense of fear? (We wonder if she will ever look out of her selfish world, or if she is to be bound within the prison of *her* thoughts for ever.) Suddenly Christ thundered at the door of her heart; *I that speak unto thee am he*. Her talk stopped, the door opened, her eyes looked out and saw him, and he became the centre of her life.

It is this Christ-centredness which is so important at the beginning of faith; and its maintenance is essential for faith's survival. Without the continuance of this Christ-centredness, the old fear will rise again. It rose again for the disciples, when they thought they were going to drown. But when Christ stood up in the midst of the storm and rebuked the outward elements, he turned to the fear which they had allowed to rage within their hearts: 'Why are ye so fearful? How is it that ye have no faith?'

When James MacDonald left Scotland many years ago on a sailing boat bound for America, the ship was caught in a storm in the Pentland Firth. Many who had cursed before were praying now, thinking that they were soon to die. One woman reproved James MacDonald for not falling on his knees like the rest. But he replied, 'Woman, I pity those who are only beginning to pray now.' He had gone beforehand to God, committing himself to his care. He could afford the luxury of sitting through the storm; he had the example of his Master who slept through one.

Do we not need to rethink our approach to maintaining faith, to banishing fear? Surely it is wrong merely to drift along until some crisis arises which drives us in fear to God. Should we not rather, as a matter of course, be trusting him; would we not then be ready in faith for any shock that might come?

Hudson Taylor tells how he was helped to change the pattern of his thinking about faith. In the year when he lost Maria he was reading Mark chapter 11 in Greek, and came across the words which he was used to seeing translated, 'Have faith in God'. But the light in which he saw these words that morning in 1870 was altogether new. The focal point was not the disciples, nor their weak and trembling faith. The focal point was the faithfulness of God. Translating the phrase *Hold the faithfulness of God*, Taylor realised that this did not point to the disciples' working up faith within themselves. It pointed rather to a going out of themselves to take hold of the faithfulness of God. Years afterwards, describing how much this realisation had come to mean to him, Taylor wrote:

Let us see that in theory we hold that God is faithful; that in daily life we count upon it; and that at all times and under all circumstances we are fully persuaded of this blessed truth.

Is this not the secret of substituting faith for fear?

Profession and Prayer

I am thine, save me.

Psalm 119:94

At a crucial time in David's rise to power, he had been gladdened to hear these words from Amasai and other fighting men: 'Thine are we, David, and on thy side thou son of Jesse'. Now, when David says 'I am thine,' he acknowledges where his own allegiance lies. Whoever we are, and whatever our situation, the question of where our allegiance really lies must face us too. Can we say 'I am thine'?

What gave reality to David's profession of allegiance was the fact that God had made him his. 'I am thine, because thou hast redeemed me.' Do *we* belong to 'the church of God, which he purchased with his own blood'? And again, 'I am thine because thou hast possessed me for thyself.' Are *we* living members of the church in which he dwells and walks? How can we judge the sincerity with which we make the profession 'I am thine'? That our sincerity will be tested we can have no doubt. The minister will be tested as to whether or not his motives are pure, in what he does in the church. The Christian teacher will be tried as to whether he or she will stand firm on Christian principles. The believing businessman will be put to the test as to whether he can maintain an unsullied profession in a wordly atmosphere.

One of the surest signs that we sincerely follow Christ

as Lord is our constant dependence on him as our Saviour. Both are brought together in David's words 'I am thine, *save me*'. Peter thought himself ready to follow his Lord to prison and to death. But his readiness to follow Christ as his Lord did not flow from his trust in him as his Saviour. He had ceased to say 'save me'; and it was not long before he was saying the opposite of 'I am thine'.

Whatever testing we may meet in the church, in our school, or in business, may these two elements be always present in our hearts. May we indeed be strong to make the profession, *I am thine*. But may we follow every profession of our allegiance with the prayer for help: *Save me*.

Treading on the Serpent

And the God of peace shall bruise Satan under your feet shortly.

Romans 16:20

The trouble in the church at Rome had a human face. There were actual people who, while using good words and fair speeches, were causing 'divisions contrary to the doctrine' which the church had been taught. But the trouble was Satanic in origin.

There were reasons why Paul wished the Roman Christians to recognise the work of Satan among them. He wished them to take the matter seriously. If allowed to go on unchecked, no doubt the effect would be what Paul feared regarding the Corinthians: 'But I fear lest, by any means, as the serpent beguiled Eve through his subtilty, so your minds should be corrupted from the simplicity that is in Christ.' Another reason was, Paul wished to warn his readers that they would not be able to deal with this difficulty in their own strength.

Having had their attention drawn to the Satanic source of their trouble, perhaps these believers would have been afraid to touch it. But Paul was telling them that they would have to deal with it. They were to put it under their feet. They were to stamp out the discord, looking to the God of peace to grant them deliverance from it.

In our own lives, when we feel the power of sin, we are to put our foot by faith on the serpent's head.

Looking to the God of peace, remembering the ancient promise that the woman's seed would bruise the serpent's head, we are to do it. It is not comfortable; we might prefer to run away; but we must do it in faith.

In our work for the kingdom of God in public, the principle is the same. When Moses' rod was changed to a serpent, his natural instinct was to flee from it. But God told him to take hold of the serpent. He had to stretch out his hand and grasp the repulsive creature. Then it became again a symbol of the authority of God, a sign of the fact that the kingdom of God would prevail against the serpent and its seed. So Moses had to go to Pharaoh's court. He had to lay upon the seed of the serpent the claims of the living God. Then, after a bondage of four hundred years, the promise was fulfilled for the Israelites in one night: 'the God of peace shall bruise Satan under your feet shortly' — that is, soon or *suddenly*.

How often in spiritual warfare, after a long campaign, there is a sudden crisis. Satanic forces, opposing the kingdom of God, are suddenly broken and retire to take up their stand on another ridge. At the closing prayer, after one of the crucial sermons prior to the revival at Cambuslang, William McCulloch asked, 'Where are the fruits of my poor labours among these people?' He did not have long to wait. The bruising of the serpent's head came suddenly, soon afterwards.

Wisdom

Give me now wisdom.

2 Chronicles 1:10

If we lack a particular physical or mental gift, we cannot be blamed for that. But if we lack wisdom, if we display a marked imbalance in our views; if we get so immersed in the details of issues that we forget the broad principles which ought to govern all we do, there is something wrong. The Scripture says, 'If any man lacks wisdom, *let him ask of God.*'

We sometimes forget that Solomon *asked* for wisdom. He had been called in providence to succeed his father David on the throne of Israel, and he felt his insufficiency. But he did not simply sit at home and mope about it; he went to Gibeon where God's tabernacle was. The one thousand sacrifices which Solomon offered there were as so many pleas to the God of heaven for help. 'In that night did God appear unto Solomon, and said unto him *Ask what I shall give thee.*'

Solomon could have asked for wealth or the life of his enemies, thinking that the granting of these would guarantee economic and military success. But he did not ask for these. In the marginal rendering of 1 Kings 3:9, he asked for *a hearing heart*. He asked for a hearing heart that, when he would feel his ignorance, he might be open to receive wisdom from above; that, when he would feel his danger, he might be guided by the God with whom his safety lay. He realised that, in facing all manner of problems, the supreme matter was to have God's help and guidance. So, what he asked was, 'Give me now wisdom'.

'The principal part of wisdom is the fear of the Lord', as Solomon was afterwards to write in Proverbs. What does this fear of God mean? How does it relate to that wisdom we need for solving the problems we meet from day to day? It is not an inherent capacity for always arriving at the right answers. God never intended us to be protected from a sense of our weakness and folly in this way. It is rather a daily dying to a sense of superior power, and a living to the grace of God. It is a continual discarding of what is carnal, and a reaching out to what is heavenly.

What blessings will we have, if we learn to look to God from day to day as Solomon did? 'Then shalt thou walk in thy way safely, and thy foot shall not stumble. When thou liest down, thou shalt not be afraid: yea, thou shalt lie down, and thy sleep shall be sweet . . . for the Lord shall be thy confidence, and shall keep thy foot from being taken.'

The Spirit of Reformation

*All scripture is given by inspiration of God, and is
profitable for doctrine, for reproof, for correction, for
instruction in righteousness.*

2 Timothy 3:16

What is the spirit of reformation? Surely it is the
willingness to be guided, in what we do and how we do
it, by the word of God.

When Knox and the other leaders of the church in
Scotland submitted the First Book of Discipline to the
Great Council of Scotland, they asked that anything in
the book which was not supported by 'God's expressed
commandment' or 'by equity and good conscience' be
noted so that it could be removed. This is the spirit of
reformation.

How far should the spirit of reformation carry us?
Perhaps there were some excesses during the sixteenth
century Reformation. When people went on the ram-
page, smashing up churches, no doubt they were going
too far; although one can understand their urge to break
free from everything connected with the dead era which
was passing away.

Did Hezekiah go too far? Was he simply wishing to
wipe out the past — or was it the true spirit of reformation which moved him when 'he brake in pieces the
brazen serpent that Moses had made; for unto those
days the children of Israel did burn incense to it: and he
called it Nehushtan' (2 Kings 18:4). Some people might

have urged him to show greater restraint; to show more regard for the people's feelings, more respect for history. But when we are really guided by the word of God we will not permit anything to come between us and God — not even something which came by divine appointment, not even something recalling a glorious deliverance in our history.

In a period of declension, the church can depart from the word of God in two ways. She may begin to deny the plain teaching of Scripture, or she may begin to hold that teaching in a way which is formal and dead. In Hezekiah's day, there was evidence of declension in both these ways. So he put a stop to heathen worship first of all. But his spirit also burned against what had become the symbol of a superstitious and sentimental regard for what God had done in the past. Hezekiah wanted to cut out everything that attracted feelings of regard and reverence which were due to God alone. So he dragged *Old Brassy* (Dr Duncan's translation of *Nehushtan*) from his pedestal and smashed him up.

The spirit of reformation is not something appropriate only to the great revivals in church history. It is something which must be maintained. How is it to be maintained? By a constant, intelligent, spiritual subjecting of all we do and the way we do it to the only standard given us by God:

All scripture is given by inspiration of God, and is profitable for doctrine, for reproof, for correction, for instruction in righteousness.

The Peacemakers

Blessed are the peacemakers: for they shall be called the children of God.

Matthew 5:9

Ecumenists seem to strive for 'peace at any price'; they seem to ignore the order established in Scripture: 'first *pure*, then peaceable'. But we must watch that, in guarding against false peace, we do not neglect the peace which God can give. That this would be dishonouring to God is clear from the fact that God has taken to himself the title 'the God of peace'.

It was not he who opened the breach between himself and his creatures, but it was he who took the initiative in seeking to heal that breach. He promised to send one whose name would be 'the Prince of peace'. When he came, God proclaimed peace in his name (Acts 10:36). It was as the God of peace that God set the seal of his acceptance on the atoning work of Christ when he raised him from the dead (Hebrews 13:20).

God has done all this for peace: what are we doing about it? At the end of his second Epistle to the Corinthians Paul writes: 'Finally brethren . . . be of one mind, live in peace'. He is not superficially plastering over the cracks in the unity of the Corinthian church. He has exposed the situation at the beginning of his first Epistle: 'There are contentions among you'. What he is saying is that believers have a duty to face the situation and to do something about it.

What can they do? Just before giving the command to live in peace Paul writes 'Be of good comfort'. Believers have a duty to live in the comfort of the gospel; they are called to 'let the peace of God rule in their hearts' (Col. 3:15). If they lived more in the atmosphere of the gospel themselves, would they not be more likely to live in peace with others?

If we do appropriate the comforts of the gospel, if we do live out the implications of the gospel in relation to others, what will we have? The glorious prospect which Paul held out to the peacemakers at Corinth was: 'And the God of love and peace will be with you'.

Blessed are the peacemakers.

Sufficient Grace

My grace is sufficient for thee.

2 Corinthians 12:9

In our desire to grow in grace and to succeed in the service of Christ, we may yearn to be lifted above those limitations which are natural, and those failures which are an inevitable feature of our service in this world. We would like to have a direct experience of abundant grace — but instead of lifting us above our limitations God sends us something which brings them painfully to our attention. He does so in order that we might look to the sufficiency of his grace. It is then, as we look to him to meet our need, that we will find his grace to abound.

Paul was lifted up to the third Heaven. But that experience of abundant grace was exceptional; he was brought down to earth again. 'And lest I should be exalted above measure through the abundance of the revelations, there was given to me a thorn in the flesh, the messenger of Satan to buffet me, lest I should be exalted above measure.'

'There was given to me.' Surely no child, unwrapping an unwanted present, could know disappointment more than this! Paul could not send his present back; he could not re-address it to someone else. This sharp and painful thing was appointed for him. What was this present? A custom-built device, designed to keep a particular member of the kingdom of heaven from being lifted up!

'For this I besought the Lord thrice.' Paul did not want this pain; he did not want to labour under this limitation; he wanted to shake off this shadow that had begun to follow him. 'And he said to me.' He did not even discuss the question of removing the thorn. He went straight on to the issue of coping with it. The will of the servant, eminent servant though he was, was to be crossed.

> *Disappointment, his appointment*
> *Change one letter, then I see*
> *That the thwarting of my purpose*
> *Is God's better will for me.*

'My grace is sufficient for thee.' Paul was not to rise above the reach of Satan; but the grace of God was to flow down to him where he was. He was to know the touch of God, at the very point where he and the kingdom of Satan were in painful contact. 'O the depth of the riches, both of the wisdom and knowledge of God! How unsearchable are His judgments, and his ways past finding out!'

Revival

I will yet for this be enquired of by the house of Israel,
to do it for them.

Ezekiel 36:37

Some readers may regard the subject of revival with
suspicion. For them 'revival' represents something
organised by men, something which is the product of
man-centred theology. However, if the term has been
cheapened in this way, it is all the more reason for us to
study carefully what Scripture says on the subject.

Ezekiel chapters 36-37 provide an ideal example of
Scripture teaching on revival. The background to this
passage tells us of the need there was that God should
revive his cause. His people had sinned, and had reaped
the fruit of their sin in a spiritual death which was
outwardly represented in their alienation from the
promised land.

But this passage also exhibits, in the clearest possible
way, the provision which would meet the church's
need. It was God's covenant with his church. And it was
a covenant which would certainly be kept by God,
though dishonoured by his church in her backslidden
state; for his glory was involved (36:21). It was a
covenant whose provisions were perfectly *suited* to the
church's need. She was defiled, but the covenant promise was 'Then will I sprinkle clean water upon you, and
ye shall be clean' (36:25). The provisions of this covenant were also *sufficient* for the church's need. As a fruit

of her backsliding, the church was languishing in despair. But here, in the word and power of God's spirit, was hope for the hopeless and life for the dead (37:1-14).

What does this lead us to? 'Thus saith the Lord God; I will yet for this be enquired of by the house of Israel, to do it for them' (36:37). There is an emphasis placed here on the fact that the church is a collective body: *the house of Israel*. This reminds us that, in all great revivals of his cause, the Lord has stirred up his people to act unitedly in pleading for his return. Thus before Pentecost: 'These all continued with one accord in prayer and supplication, with the women' (Acts 1:14).

In the eighteenth century there was more than one agreement, drawn up among Christians in different countries and from different denominations, to pray unitedly for this reviving power. Nor were such Concerts for Prayer unrelated to the revivals which the church knew then. In recent years some believers have set aside a little time on Saturday evenings to pray for such revival again. Would others feel inclined to do the same?

Rest

Return unto thy rest, O my soul.

Psalm 116:7

When other aspects of creation had been finished, man was called into existence to rest in what God had done. In the realm of redemption, too, the work is only God's. It is because Christ said once 'It is finished' that he says to us every day, 'Come to me, and I will give you rest'.

It seems, from verse 11, that it was unbelief which robbed the Psalmist of his rest. But unbelief can come to us in various ways. We may become too worried about food and clothing, about our own and our family's tomorrow. Perhaps we are being called to serve God, and are refusing to rest in his will because of an undue obsession with our inability. Or perhaps we are simply harassed, with too much work to do. How many devices Satan has to rob us of that rest which is our right, through faith in Christ! But now, as the Psalmist returns to his rest, he recognises that his soul had been set apart for this rest. 'Return to *thy* rest, O my soul.'

What spirit will characterise the soul that is returning to its rest? As in every fresh development in the church's spiritual experience, there is new faith. 'I believed, therefore have I spoken.' His heart has suffered enough from the plague of unbelief, that spirit of refusing to receive. Now there is faith; 'I will take the cup of salvation'. He is yet to receive *glory* from God;

what more heavenly activity for him in time than to stretch out his hand for *grace*?

There is new gratitude. 'I love the Lord, because he hath heard my voice . . . I will offer to thee the sacrifice of thanksgiving.' What thankfulness must have filled the heart of Thomas when his soul returned to its rest at the feet of his Saviour: 'My Lord and my God'!

There is also new obedience: 'O Lord, truly I am thy servant . . . I will pay my vows unto the Lord now in the presence of all his people, in the courts of the Lord's house, in the midst of thee, O Jerusalem.'

O my soul, join with all of God's believing, thankful and obedient people. *Return unto thy rest, O my soul.*

Soldiers

The battle is not yours, but God's.

2 Chronicles 20:15

Timothy was addressed as a soldier: 'Endure hardness, as a good soldier of Jesus Christ'. This is something which is not restricted to ministers. All Christians are exhorted, 'Put on the whole armour of God, that ye may be able to stand against the wiles of the devil' (Eph. 5:11).

If we have been born into the kingdom of Heaven, we will know already that there is a war on. But we need to be reminded from time to time that there is no truce between the kingdom of Satan and the kingdom of God's dear son. We think sadly of David, remembering how the turn of the year caught him off his guard. At the time 'when kings go forth to battle' the king of Israel was lying on his bed at Jerusalem. The tragedy of this great warrior being caught unguarded ought to make us weep. It should also make us watch, in case Satan gets an advantage over us as well. How may we know if we are ready for the conflict?

Jehoshaphat, another Old Testament king, was confronted by an enemy that was numerous, powerful, and determined to destroy. But when he went out to battle, his eye was not on his enemy but on his God: 'Art not thou God in heaven and rulest not thou over all the kingdoms of the heathen, and in thine hand is there not power and might, so that none is able to withstand thee?' Jehoshaphat had faith.

He also had the spirit of prayer: 'O, our God, wilt thou not judge them?' Where there are these two, the spirit of praise cannot be far behind. In the case of Jehoshaphat and his army, the spirit ot praise, in fact, went before victory: 'And when they began to sing and to praise, the Lord set ambushments against their enemies.'

One essential feature of a successful army is, unity. This makes it more effective as a body, and the safety of each individual member is much increased. Not that the church has the hard, impressive appearance of a normal fighting force. 2 Chronicles 20:13 paints a different picture from that: 'All Judah stood before the Lord with their little ones, their wives and their children.' They appear so exposed and so vulnerable! But they stand there, not as before their enemy, but as 'before the Lord'. They know that their lives are in Jehovah's hand, and that the issue in the approaching battle lies with him. They are as one great family of God, and on his love and his protection they depend.

What a blessing if the church today were more like that — indulging no illusions about the opposition we face, yet taking our stand together on the faithfulness of God.

He leadeth Me

The Lord is my shepherd; I shall not want. He maketh me to lie down in green pastures; He leadeth me beside the still waters.

Psalm 23:1-2

If you are trusting in Christ, you know the shepherd of whom David is speaking here. Then you, too, can say 'He leadeth me'. In this Psalm, David speaks of some of the blessings to which Christ leads his flock. What are they?

You have *a provision* for the way. 'He maketh me to lie down in green pastures; he leadeth me beside the still waters . . . Thou preparest a table before me.' You may feel at times that God cannot provide for you. But he sent a provision to Elijah even in a time of drought, though he had to recruit ravens to send it.

You have *protection* along the way: protection in the face of enemies (v.5) and in the face of death (v.4). In spite of these threats David could say 'Thou art with me'. Hezekiah knew that he and his people had this protection, even though the Assyrian army was marching towards them. 'Be strong and courageous,' he said to his people. 'With us is the Lord our God to help us, and to fight our battles.'

You have a glorious *prospect* at the end of the way. As a result of the death of the shepherd, prophesied in Psalm 22, his flock can even now 'rejoice in hope of the glory of God'. 'I will dwell in the house of the Lord forever.'

All these blessings you have in a *personal* way. The Lord is *my* shepherd. He leadeth *me*.

Many years ago a Scottish shepherd boy, Jamie, lay ill and dying in his cottage. His employer asked a Christian to call at the shepherd boy's home. This visitor spoke to Jamie about sheep, and then told him of a shepherd he knew who had a great many sheep and lambs — he spoke to Jamie about Christ. He told him that if he received Jesus as his Saviour, he would then be able to say 'The Lord is my shepherd'. To help the boy remember the words the visitor counted them out, one on each knuckle. The next day this man returned and asked Jamie's mother how her boy was. Jamie's mother was in tears. 'Jamie's gone,' she said.

'And how did he die?' the man asked.

'He died with his finger on the fourth knuckle,' Jamie's mother replied.

This story was told to children in Spurgeon's church, and among the children who heard it was a three year old boy called Stanley. Some time after this, Spurgeon died. When Stanley met the man who had told him this story, he said to him 'Mr Spurgeon has died, and gone to heaven on the fourth knuckle.'

What a full provision in an empty world, what sure protection in a dangerous world, what a glorious prospect in a dark world; and how personally all these blessings are enjoyed by us when we say: *He leadeth me*.